Than

GEOFFREY CULVERWELL was born in Bristol of
an English father and a Norwegian mother.
He spent his early childhood in Bath before
moving to the New Forest where his family
lived for fifteen years. He was educated at
Harrow and Trinity College, Dublin, and
then spent some months in Italy before
returning to London where he joined
Sotheby's as a trainee. He later became a
freelance translator and travelled extensively
before settling in Buckinghamshire.

THANK YOU SO MUCH

Geoffrey Culverwell

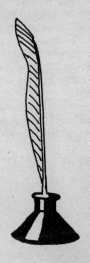

HEADLINE

ISBN: 0 7472 3071 4

HEADLINE BOOK PUBLISHING PLC
Headline House
79 Great Titchfield Street
London W1P 7FN

Typesetting by Action Typesetting Ltd, Gloucester
Printed & Bound by Wm Collins, Glasgow

What the critics say:

'Really puts the boot in' *The British Stormtrooper*

'Føll øf useføl tøps' *Skandinaviske Døgblødet*

'Miraculous' *Courier de Lourdes*

'A dialectic treatise that reveals the decadent
nature of capitalist bourgeois society'
The Voice of Pyongyang

'Riveting' *Metalworker's Review*

'A gross provocation' *Pravda*

Dear Reader,

Thank you for buying my book. If you didn't buy it yourself, thank you for having such generous and perspicacious friends. If you nicked it, then words fail me.

> Your humble and obedient servant,
>   The Author

Dear Reader who bought,

Thank you for swelling my royalties.
>   Yours lovingly,
>   The Author

Dear Reader who didn't,
What's so wrong with buying your own copy, cheapskate?
>   Yours graspingly,
>   The Author

Dear Kleptomaniac,
All thieves should be made honorary citizens of Saudi Arabia.
>   Yours sincerely,
>   Edwina Currie

Prologue

Many years ago, long before spaghetti came in tins, people wrote real letters and the mailcoaches of Olde England actually carried mail rather than details of the latest Reader's Digest prize competition. The advent of the telephone has changed all that, however, and letter-writing, which never fully recovered from the untimely death of Madame de Sévigné in 1696, now threatens to go the same way as shell grottoes and stumpwork. Apart from brief flurries of correspondence with the Gas Board or Peter Jones' accounts department and the annual newsletter to displaced Brits in far-off climes, most people's experience of letter-writing nowadays is restricted to the thank-you letter. But even this genre, the last relic of a proud literary tradition, has become a duty rather than a pleasure, a chore rather than an art, which explains all those decidedly wooden offerings that hover briefly over the doormat before landing in the bin.

What many people still fail to realize is that the most important element of the thank-you letter is its recipient and that every writer is duty-bound to ensure that his or her letter makes pleasant reading. As we shall see later, the latter requirement may involve indulging in a measure of duplicity and dissimulation, but when it comes to writing thank-you letters the ends more than justify the means. It is certainly not my intention to flood the sorting offices of the nation with the kind of letter likely to create lengthy queues outside the local confessional or to cause a sudden upsurge in the use of casual perjury, but the white lie has always been a vital weapon in man's social armoury: Casanova probably signed all his letters 'Yours faithfully' and *he* never seemed to be short of friends. Whether he ever actually got round to writing all his thank-you letters is quite another matter, of course, but then nobody's perfect . . .

'A letter does not blush'.

CICERO, Epistolae ad Atticum

Grace

Thank you for the world so sweet,
Thank you for the food we eat,
Thank you for the birds that sing,
Thank you God for everything.

And Disfavour

I hate school and I hate my little sister;
I hate cabbage and pilchards.
I hate the Nolan sisters.
If I don't get a BMX bike for my birthday
You're in big trouble.

THE FIRST COMMANDMENT

THOU SHALT NOT REPEAT A SUCCESS

Some recipients have a nasty habit of hoarding letters or, even worse, circulating particularly entertaining ones amongst family and friends. To be caught sending the same thank-you letter to several people is tantamount to committing social seppuku.

THE SECOND COMMANDMENT

THOU SHALT USE A FOUNTAIN PEN

(or at least one of those crafty Japanese substitutes)

This applies particularly to formal letters: it creates a much better impression than a fluff-covered Bic with a penchant for blobs. Do not however, use a fountain pen for the envelope since British postmen like to rinse all letters in rainwater before delivering them.

If a picture painted a thousand words, then would not the brush be mightier than the pen?

"Never bore people by writing letters that drag on..."
Anon. Anon. Anon.

Discretion is the better part of letter-writing.

Punctuation is the politeness of kings.

Dear Paul,
Thanks for the epistle.
Yours faithfully,
Diana and all at Ephesus.

The wages of social truth are social death.

A diplomatic thank-you letter is like a well-designed girdle: all-embracing yet all-concealing.

The quality of *merci* ain't half strained.

Honi soit qui mal y écrit

The set piece

*'Miss Otis regrets. . .
but sends thanks all the same'.*

There is a great deal to be said for that last relic of the 'auld dacency', the properly printed invitation or 'stiffy'. Apart from adding lustre to the county mantelpiece, it gives its recipients ample time in which to decide whether to accept or decline and also allows them to express their thanks in accordance with a formula that can conceal the truth more effectively than any door-to-door salesman. The key element in this formula is the use of the disembodied third person, which means we can all salve our consciences by indulging in a temporary bout of schizophrenia: we can pretend that it is some uncontrollable alter ego who is thanking the Australian cultural attaché for his kind invitation to an exhibition of aborigine bark paintings, but declining it due to some prior and totally fictitious engagement. This same alter ego can graciously express our thanks to Lady Snodgrass for her kind invitation to a dinner party, which we know from bitter experience will be a fatal combination of indigestion and boredom, and then wriggle out of it without batting an eyelid. We have all had good reason to be thankful for those magic letters *R.S.V.P.*, which still continue to provide such a convenient and acceptable means of slaloming through the cowpats of life.

'For this relief, much thanks.'
SHAKESPEARE, *Hamlet*

15

His Excellency the British Ambassador
and
Lady Strangeways
thank
His Excellency the Mongolian
Ambassador
and
Madame Dung
for their kind invitation to a
National Motherhood Day Reception
at the Mongolian Embassy
but regret that
they will be unable to attend

EDITH STRANGEWAYS IS HAPPY TO ANNOUNCE that she has finally persuaded her husband to go away on holiday in May with the specific intention of avoiding not only Mongolian National Motherhood day (four ghastly hours of speeches, folk dancing and lamb stew), but also Albanian Independence Day (speeches and slides of smiling tractor drivers, the high spot of which was provided last year by the Egyptian Ambassador's wife, a lady of ample proportions, who disgraced herself by falling noisily asleep and smothering the first Secretary) and that extraordinary bunfight held by the Gabonese Ambassador to celebrate the eradication of the mosquito (coconut segments on sticks and slices of green banana in peanut sauce, which may well do more to explain the mass flight of the mosquito than any amount of DDT). In the meantime, she is seriously considering getting her own back next year by erecting a maypole on the Embassy lawn and importing a troupe of marathon Morris dancers.

Sir Harold and Lady Bluejohn
thank Colonel and Mrs Skipton-Fell
for their kind invitation
to the wedding
of their daughter Amanda,
but regret that
they are unable to attend.

SIR HAROLD AND LADY BLUEJOHN have finally cottoned on to the fact that owning a large house in a village with no hotels has one very unfortunate consequence: it unleashes a flood of invitations from people they barely know who are desperately seeking accommodation for their more feeble-minded relations. They are still haunted by the memory of that frightful menagerie wished on them for Amanda's 21st birthday. How could they possibly forget the aunt with the incontinent poodle, the vegetarian cousin and the girl with pink hair who threw up on the bootscraper? They have learnt their lesson and are beating a strategic retreat to the South of France.

*Sir Ronald and Lady Luce-Dencher
thank the Chairman
and Committee of
the Anglo-Ukrainian Friendship League
for their kind invitation to
an exhibition of folk dancing
and handicrafts
in Ealing Town Hall,
but regret that they
will be unable to attend.*

DEAR GOD — a whole evening of painted eggs and slapped thighs. We cannot think of a more deadly combination. Lady Luce-Dencher is still recovering from all those ghastly Filipinos in the Festival Hall, who started off playing nose-flutes and ended up three hours later trying to bash each other noisily to death with bamboo poles. The thought of hordes of buxom peasant girls in swirling petticoats shrieking down off the steppes into Ealing Town Hall and then being flung about by men in funny hats to the sound of balalaikas is really too much. Sir Colin is quite attracted by the thought of all those thighs, but her Ladyship has put her foot down and said she would rather stay home and watch telly.

Mr and Mrs George Crosse
thank the Rev. Oscar Knelton-Praed
for his kind invitation to
a cheese and wine party
in the crypt of
St Ethelburga's Church
and have much pleasure
in accepting.

NEITHER OF US can think of anything worse than being trapped in a crypt for two hours with a case of Algerian Beaujolais, but one of the penalties of living next door to the church, apart from bloody bell-ringing practice every Friday, is being sitting ducks for all your crackpot get-togethers. We tried hiding last year with all the curtains drawn, but your stoat-faced wife just happened to pop in in case we'd forgotten. I don't mind risking life and limb trying to decorate the organ-loft with vegetable marrows for Harvest Festival, or even knitting recycled blankets for the Third World, but I do draw the line at frontal assault by that dreadful red-faced verger, who invariably sprays me with pieces of Tesco camembert like a cross between a Kalashnikov and an enraged llama. George is seriously considering becoming a Mormon.

THE THIRD COMMANDMENT

THOU SHALT NOT LEAVE LARGE EXPANSES OF VIRGIN PAPER

If you have trouble-fulfilling your bread-and-butter quota, either buy smaller writing paper or cultivate larger handwriting: there is no more depressing sight than a letter resembling either an optician's chart or a gravestone with a four-line epitaph.

THE FOURTH COMMANDMENT

THOU SHALT STRIVE FOR LEGIBILITY

The judicious extrusion of words may help fill the page, but not everyone is a trained code-breaker. If, however, it is of no concern to you whether the contents can be read of not, then at least make sure that there is a liberal scattering of exclamation marks (a feature normally to be avoided in thank-you letters). In this way your reader will gain the impression that he or she has received a witty and ecstatic outpouring of thanks.

Hatch, match and despatch

'Life is just a bowl of . . . raspberries.'

Every major hiccup in life's stately progress is accompanied not only by a suitable announcement in *The Times* (or, at a pinch, *The Daily Telegraph*), but also by an influx of letters containing appropriate expressions of congratulation or commiseration, however contrived.

In the event of shotgun weddings, births the wrong side of the blanket and wife murder the distinction between the two emotions may become a trifle blurred in the writer's mind, but the social niceties still have to be observed . . . And these letters all have to be acknowledged, of course. In the case of births this normally poses no problem: all that is required is a grateful acknowledgement of the original letter and suitable expressions of thanks for the writer's good wishes. The same formula can also be applied on the occasion of an engagement, assuming, of course, that the wedding has not been called off in the interim due to incompatibility, infidelity or disease of an intimate and highly contagious nature, but when it comes to replying to 'dead letters', particularly from people with whom the bereaved is only vaguely familiar or may even actively dislike, there is no alternative to seeking refuge in a safe yet socially acceptable combination of platitude and harmless cliché. How else can anyone decently reply to a letter from someone of whom the late lamented consistently said 'Over my dead body will that person ever enter this house'?

> 'A lie which is half a truth is ever the blackest of lies'.
> TENNYSON, *The Grandmother*

French letters can be a *merci* business.

Better one heavenly page than a whole celestial quire.

A letter is a lovesome thing, God wot.

When writing thank-you letters, take a tip from the beauticians of Saudi Arabia and draw a veil over the bad bits.

One man's gloss is another man's gain.

The way to a man's heart is through his ego.

Blessed are those who write letters to maiden aunts for they shall inherit.

Dear Jane,

Thank you so much for the sweet letter you sent me in hospital. Rodney and I are both thrilled and so is Benedict, who cannot wait to play with his little sister. We have decided to call her Dorothy after Rodney's aunt, but we haven't yet made up our minds about her middle names. I got home yesterday and I now have a fortnight's grace while the maternity nurse is in residence and then I shall be on my own. You must come round one evening and see us. It really was very kind of you to have thought of writing. Again, many thanks.

Love,
Amanda

Dear Jane,

I know you're hell bent on being a godmother, but over my dead body as I going to have another of Rodney's impoverished ex's lurking round the house waving bits of Mothercare plastic and making silly noises. It was bad enough having that dreadful Clare and Joanna jostling for position at the font during Benedict's christening and making sheep's eyes at Rodney. Benedict keeps on asking me when I'm going to take the baby back to the hospital. I quite understand how he feels. I hate the name Dorothy; I think it's dreadfully common, but Aunt Dorothy *is* enormously rich and, what is even more important, she's also unmarried. It's just a pity the old bag didn't cough up for a full month's worth of maternity nursing, but then all Rodney's family are incredibly mean.

Amanda

Dear Caroline,

Thank you so much for your nice letter. You weren't the only one to be taken by surprise — Mummy and Daddy are still in a state of shock and even I can't believe it's really happening. We haven't fixed a date yet for the wedding, but it looks as though it'll have to be March if Tim can get the time off — I do hope you'll be around. As you can imagine; life's pretty hectic at the moment with all the arrangements, but Tim has got masses of nieces and nephews and so at least there isn't going to be any shortage of bridesmaids and pages! Again many thanks for the letter and please give my regards to your parents.

Much love,
Liza.

Dear Caroline,

We'd laid bets on you being the first to write — Tim maintains that the only breakfast-time noises in the Pullen-Fawcett household are your father munching through his corn flakes and you and your mother rustling through the social undergrowth of *The Times* like a pair of hyperactive spaniels. I know that your families are best friends and that your mother has been trying to marry you off from an early age (it would also appear that you cottoned onto the idea fairly quickly and spent your formative years trying to lure Tim into the shrubbery to play doctors and nurses), but I also know you're the most appalling gossip, which is why we had to keep the whole thing such a dark secret, even from my parents. I'm trying to fix the wedding for March because I hate skiing and it's the best way I can think of to sabotage Tim's annual orgy at Verbier and reduce the Hoorah Henry quota at the reception. If I do a quick outflanking manoeuvre and get all his little nephews and nieces worked up at the prospect of a March wedding, I'm relying on the fact that he won't have the heart to disappoint them by altering the date. Sorry to have deprived you and your mother of a matrimonial stand-by, but all's fair in love and war and if you're really desperate to get married, take a tip from me and start divorce proceedings against your mother.

Liza.

Dear Miss Brown,

Thank you so much for the kind letter you sent after George's death. You are quite right, I do miss him dreadfully, but as you so wisely pointed out, life must go on and time is a great healer. It has been a great source of comfort to me reading the many letters I have received from people I hardly knew, but who were obviously very close to my late husband. It was very thoughtful of you to write and I will certainly drop in for tea if I'm ever passing through Dollis Hill. In the meantime, many thanks for your condolences and I hope all goes well for you in the future.

Yours,
Blanche Crofton

Dear Miss Brown,

Thank you for yet another extract from the Wonder Book of Clichés. I can't work out whether you're the elderly spinster with yellow teeth and a moustache who lurked behind the filing cabinets in a haze of cigarette smoke or the bleach-blonde typist with large breasts who accompanied George on his so-called business trip to Hamburg last winter, but it doesn't really matter. I must confess, however, that I'm amazed at the number of unknown females who have written to me; I always knew my husband was a randy old goat, but I'm now beginning to understand why he had a heart attack. The only great healer I know is penicillin and even that couldn't cure George's venereal disease; if you're the flighty blonde you're going to be remembering George for much longer than you anticipated, and if you're the elderly spinster I hope you washed the coffee mugs up properly or there are going to be raised eyebrows at the clinic.

Mrs Crofton

P.S.   Where, in God's name, is Dollis Hill?

THE FIFTH COMMANDMENT

THOU SHALT NOT BEGIN WITH THE WORDS

'This is just a short note to say thank you . . .'

Although it is true that the majority of thank-you letters contain more padding than the average Swiss duvet, this opening gambit is altogether too blatant and too hackneyed to be acceptable. Besides, it also gives the game away.

THE SIXTH COMMANDMENT

THOU SHALT START AS THOU MEANETH TO CONTINUE

If you write a thank-you letter once, then people will always expect one and will become unreasonably suspicious and aggrieved should they fail to receive one on later occasions. This affliction is known as Basildon bondage and the only known cure for it is amputation.

Confucius, he say: man who writes sweet and sour thank-you letters will get hit on head with wok.

> 'Tis better to lie and bear the shame,
> Than tell the truth and get the blame.
> *Anon*

When writing thank-you letters, take a leaf out of Ruth's book and cut the corn.

Truth in a letter is like an iceberg in an ocean: two-thirds of it are hidden.

Letters pray for the gift of eloquence.

Write in haste, repent at leisure.

The thank-you letter: a thing of duty and a joy forever.

The acknowledgement

'Birds do it,
Bees do it . . .
We should all do it sometime.'

There are certain occasions when even mature adults hear a still, small, voice from their childhood saying, 'You really ought to write'. The fruits of the ensuing Pavlovian reflex, which takes the form of letters acknowledging everything from another letter to a potted plant, are also a useful way of piling up halo points because they are an optional extra on the social menu. There is always the alternative of a telephone call, but where letters score is the way in which they keep their target at arm's length, thereby ensuring that (a) one's telephone bill remains slightly lower than the Guatemalan GNP and (b) there is less likelihood of any unwanted follow-on ('I'm so glad you've rung. I've lost your number and I was wondering whether you'd like to come to see the Winbledon Operatic Society doing "Naughty Marietta" in aid of the local play group. I've been helping do the costumes and it should be great fun...'). Because such letters are frequently regarded as an unexpected bonus by their recipients, they are the ones most likely to stick in people's minds, giving rise to remarks such as 'Thank you so much for your nice letter: you really shouldn't have bothered' and enabling the assiduous thank-you letter writer to bathe in a warm, self-righteous glow.

Gratitude is a fruit of great cultivation; you do not find it among gross people'.

SAMUEL JOHNSON, *Tour to the Hebrides*

Dear Captain Greaves,

Thank you so much for taking me round your garden last Sunday and also for showing me your amazing collection of model soldiers which I'd heard so much about from the Rowlands. It was extremely kind of you to go to all that trouble. I'm sorry that I couldn't stay longer, but I had to get back to London. I hope we meet again the next time I'm down in Wiltshire. In the meantime, again very many thanks for a fascinating afternoon.

       Yours sincerely,
        Toby Gardner

Dear Captain Greaves,

Before you came to lunch with the Rowlands they warned me about your twin obsessions, but I never imagined you'd interpret my polite social noises as signs of interest: I thought that wild gleam was just the light bouncing off your glass eye. Despite my name, I cannot distinguish between a hernia and a wisteria and, like all right-minded people, I gave up playing with toy soldiers at the age of twelve, but I still found myself being dragged off to your house and trailed through acres of dripping shrubbery like a trainee bloodhound. When both my shoes and my mind had reached saturation point I was frog-marched indoors to gaze at acres of chipboard covered in tiny figures re-enacting the Peninsula War. Humouring one's friends' neighbours is one thing, but being held hostage for a whole afternoon by a retarded army officer with green fingers is quite another. I shall wait until you've been committed before I visit the Rowlands again.

Yours sincerely,
Toby Gardner

Dear Miss Smith,

This is just a short note to say thank you very much for bring round that rubber plant — how clever of you to remember me admiring it at the bank last Christmas. It really was extremely kind of you — I've put it in the hall and it looks very handsome. I always think it's nice to have one good-sized plant in a house. Again many thanks,

Yours sincerely,
Myrtle Fairweather

Dear Miss Smith,

So much for light social banter with my husband's staff at the Christmas cocktail party... When I told you I was very fond of plants and that I thought it was a shame the bank threw them out after they'd grown too large, I never dreamed that in early January I would be opening my front door to let in a fully-grown tree with a small spinster attached. The hall now looks like a set from *Carry on Up the Jungle* and the cats are still hiding under the sofa — Lord knows how you managed to get the bloody thing onto a bus. I hope you've got the message about the 'one good-sized plant' or I shall have to talk seriously to my husband about that awful Swiss cheese plant outside his office, in case that boards the No. 49 as well. I have no intention of running a home for retired Triffids.

Yours sincerely,
Myrtle Fairweather

Dear Mrs Curwen,

Thank you so much for having Dai to stay over the Bank Holiday weekend. It really was very kind of you. He had a wonderful time and thoroughly enjoyed himself — I only hope he wasn't too much trouble. I must say he's full of stories about the things that he and Michael got up to in London! We must try and fix a date when Michael can come and stay with us down in Wales. In the meantime, again many thanks for everything and I look forward to seeing you at the beginning of next term. Dai himself should be writing shortly.

        Yours sincerely,
          Myfanwy Evans

Dear Mrs Curwen,

I hate to think what happened in London; Dai has told me practically nothing, but his conduct has definitely taken a turn for the worse. We had the most dreadful row outside the local post office after he'd called poor Miss Jones a silly old bag and told her to get stuffed (or words to that effect) just because she didn't stock some obscure architectural magazine called *Penthouse*. It was the first time in my life that I'd been grateful for her being deaf as a post. I think the high spot of his stay with you, apart from having his ears pierced and getting that tattoo done, was the fact that he didn't have to go to chapel on Sunday (if he'd only told me you were Jewish I wouldn't have sent all those Easter eggs and that side of ham). From my point of view, the one positive thing to emerge from his stay in London is that he's suddenly developed an interest in model-making — he's bought enough tubes of glue to build a full-scale replica of Cader Idris and spends hours in his bedroom. I just hope his cold gets better soon.

Yours sincerely,
Myfanwy Evans

Dear Susan,

Thank you so much for the beautiful flowers you sent me in hospital. The op was a complete success and it's wonderful being able to breathe properly at last — the only drag was not being allowed visitors. The weather here is fantastic and I'm having a great time. I'll give you a ring when I get back and we must meet for lunch. Again many thanks and sorry for not writing sooner. Love Shirley.

Dear Snoop,

Trust you to ferret out which hospital I was in — you must have been a TV detector van in another life. I realized that I wouldn't be able to keep it a secret for ever, but to get a bunch of wilting daffs from you before I'd even had the bloody operation has to be some sort of record. I told all my friends that I'd gone in to have surgery on a deviated septum, but I've no doubt that you've been regaling people with lurid tales about my nose-job. Thank God I managed to persuade the doctors not to let in any visitors without my permission — I woke up looking like a cross between the Curse of the Mummy's Tomb and a mugging victim. I'd hoped the bruises would subside fairly quickly and my face would stop looking like an Impressionist sunset, but when I was told how long it was going to take I decided to go away and get a tan rather than be the target of endless gossip. Anyway, when I get back I shall be brown and you'll still be as white as a camembert.

Shirley

Dear Aunt Maud,

Thank you so much for your letter. It really is very kind of you to be so concerned about William, but the doctors are very pleased with his progress and say that he'll be up and about any day now. As I mentioned in my last letter, his operation had really nothing at all to do with those game pies you so kindly sent him for his birthday, so please don't worry yourself on that account. We will try to come up and visit you when the weather gets better, but until then I hope that you keep well and please make sure you look after yourself properly. Alasdair was thrilled with the sweater you knitted for him and will be writing shortly.

Much love,
Fiona.

Dear Aunt Maud,

Not another bloody letter droning on about murdering your favourite nephew. That makes four this month. It *is* true that your parcel took five weeks to get here because you'd got the address wrong and it is equally true that we were away the weekend it arrived and that the neighbour's dachshund had to be rushed to the vet's to have its stomach pumped, but how could game pies, however stinking, possibly cause piles? Either you've been at the whisky again or it's time mother put you into a home. Mind you, if I spent half the year buried in a snowdrift in the middle of Scotland I think I'd probably start hitting the bottle. Alasdair is now fifteen and plays rugger for his school; he is not too keen on sweaters covered in fluffy bunnies.

Fiona.

THE SEVENTH COMMANDMENT

THOU SHALT NOT OVERGILD THE LILY

'Phrases like 'the most wonderful' and 'the most delicious' may be acceptable on the other side of the Atlantic (where they frequently compose letters in the key of 'Gee!'), but most Britons quite understandably equate 'gilt' with 'guilt' or, at best, insincerity. Copious underlining should be similarly avoided.

THE EIGHTH COMMANDMENT

THOU SHALT USE PLENTY OF ADJECTIVES

The adjective is to thank-you letters what fibre is to intestines: it aids digestion. Do not overdo things, however, since no one appreciates either flatulence or diarrhoea. Judicious doses of *Roget's Thesaurus* can work wonders in this respect.

Noblesse oblige

'Show me the way to go home,
I'm tired and . . .
Thoroughly cheesed off'.

One of the many potential booby prizes in life's great bran tub is the invitation that can't be turned down. After someone else has had the decency to arrange for your inclusion in a house-party in one of the remoter corners of this scepter'd isle, how can you possibly refuse, even if it does mean staying in a house with a worse reputation for discomfort and food poisoning than the average Greek hotel? Equally, how can you turn down an invitation to a wedding reception on the grounds that the prospective bride's family all turned up at the engagement party wearing Hush Puppies, thereby causing grave offence to the groom's family, whom you've known for years? The answer, of course, is that you can't, or rather shouldn't. However, having acted possibly against your better judgment and then had your worst suspicions confirmed, how do you write a gracious thank-you letter? In the case of a house-party, if the friends of the people with whom you were staying really are your friends, then you have to keep your fingers crossed (that way it doesn't count) and turn the whole thing upside down: if the food was inedible, lavish praise on the *delicious* dinner; if your hostess's aged labrador peed against your left leg within minutes of your arrival, make allusions to the warmth of his welcome, and if the bedroom was not only freezing but damp as well, remark that you slept like a log (gloss over the fact that the log metaphor also extended to the mould on the duvet cover). When thanking for a disastrous wedding reception, on the other hand, the most important thing to remember is that the bride's mother probably hasn't got a blind idea who you are (an illegible signature can also be of great use in this respect) and that if you write your letter quickly enough it will be lost in the crowd anyway. This being the case, it doesn't really matter what you write on such occasions.

> 'And to give thanks is good, and to forgive'.
> SWINBURNE, *Ave Atque Vale*

Two swallows do not make a summer, nor two lines a letter.

In thank-you letters, as in Christmas carols, all hosts are angelic.

Confucius, he say: man who writes twice with forked pen should take out third party insurance.

Better to sit on a fence than to cause it.

Never write wrongs in a thank-you letter.

Writing thank-you letters is like prospecting for oil: you have to do an awful lot of boring before you get it right.

Reading thank-you letters is like mining for diamonds: you've got to plough through a great deal of dross before you find a gem.

What the pen don't write the heart won't grieve for.

One letter is worth a thousand words.

The object of a thank-you letter is more important than the subject.

Dear Mrs Browne-Smythe,

Thank you so much for the super reception that you gave for Nigel and Denise, which I enjoyed enormously. I thought that the church was looking wonderful and the bride looked absolutely radiant; I loved her dress. It was just a shame about the weather, but I don't think even that succeeded in dampening anyone's enthusiasm! It was also great fun meeting so many of Denise's friends; in fact, all in all, it couldn't have been a more enjoyable occasion. I'm sorry I wasn't able to thank you and your husband in person, but I really did enjoy myself very much indeed.

Yours sincerely,

Clare Williamson

Dear Mrs Brown with an 'e'-hypen-Smith,

That's a suspicious name if ever I heard one, but hardly surprising since you're that girl's mother. Three long years I went out with Nigel and then along comes your trollop of a daughter and before you can say 'knife' (and God knows I've said it often enough) they're getting married. The church flowers looked just as though the Esher WI had been put in charge of a Mafia boss's funeral and I've never seen so much Crimplene and polyester since I looked at the daily's Littlewoods catalogue. The best moment was when the heavens opened up in the middle of the church photographs and made her dress cling to the bulge. I bet you get *that* airbrushed out of the proofs. It was hardly surprising that 90% of the male guests were Denise's ex-boyfriends; just trust that twit Nigel to be the one to get caught. I left early, having got the most splitting headache from that revolting Spanish champagne and violent food poisoning from a partially defrosted sausage roll, but some girl very kindly sponged down my dress and gave me a lift back to London. She used to work for your husband and said she was going with him to Paris on a business trip next weekend. Serves you bloody well right.

Clare

Dear Lady Crudginton,

What a super weekend! Thank you so much for having invited Roger and me to stay for the Brockley Hunt Ball. It really was extremely kind of you and we both had a wonderful time. The dinner party you gave before the dance was enormous fun (I didn't have any room for the breakfast kedgeree at all!) and I felt very privileged at having been seated next to your husband; he certainly has the most wonderful fund of stories. I only hope that we didn't wake you up when we got back; I'm afraid it *was* rather late. I'm sorry that we had to leave early on Sunday, but we had promised Roger's mother that we'd drop in and see her on our way back to London. I hope that you and Lord Crudgington manage to shake off your colds, but in the meantime again many thanks for a memorable weekend.

   Yours,
    Daphne Hartington

Dear Lady Crudgington,

God, what a grim weekend! I'd been warned that your house was the coldest in Northants and it's true. It wouldn't have been so bad if there'd been something to eat, but there was mould on the four chocolate biscuits produced at teatime and I found a dead spider in the pre-dinner peanuts. As if that wasn't bad enough, your husband and that appalling farmer with halitosis managed to polish everything off at dinner before I even got a look-in; it was like sitting between two Hoovers on heat. Incidentally, I think that someone should investigate your husband's unhealthy obsession with the tribal initiation rites of pre-war Japukaland. Roger and I were so hungry after dinner that we were reduced to arm-wrestling each other for the travel sweets in the car and then spent an entire night roaming the marquee in a vain search for kedgeree. When we got back and Roger woke up the dogs by tripping over the tigerskin and almost knocking himself out on the elephant's foot umbrella stand, it was probably because he was dizzy from lack of food. Our beds were so damp that I diagnosed the onset of hypothermia and threatened Roger with divorce if he didn't take me away immediately after breakfast. I'm not surprised that you and your husband suffer from dewdrops quivering constantly at the end of your noses; I'm just amazed they don't freeze.

Never again,
Daphne Hartington

Dear Countess Vongole,

Very many thanks for all the kindness and hospitality which you showed Peter and me while we were in Rome — I cannot imagine anyone having a better introduction to the 'Eternal City' than the one you gave us. You did so much for us that I really don't know where to begin — I only hope we didn't disrupt your life totally during our stay. Please thank Alfredo very much for chauffeuring us around so kindly (I don't think there can be a single church or monument which we left unvisited!) and also for taking us to the airport. We had a very uneventful flight back to England and are now busy preparing for Christmas. Aunt Edith sends you her love and hopes that you will come and stay with her soon; if you do, please let us know so that we can spend a few days together in London. In the meantime, again many thanks from us both,

> Yours sincerely,
> Rowena Leadbetter

Dear Countess Vongole,

When dear Aunt Edith said we simply had to look up an old schoolfriend of hers who lived in Rome, I never dreamed we would end up being whisked out of our hotel and installed in a crumbling palazzo with hot water on alternate days. It really was extremely kind of you, but staying with an 82-year old countess and her 60-year old retainer (who drives like Nicky Lauda on amphetamines) did have its drawbacks. Religion has never loomed large in my life, but I lit a candle to St Christopher in every single church we visited, offering up a silent prayer that Alfredo wouldn't kill us all before the next one. It was also very sweet of you to persuade poor old Serafina to cook us a proper English breakfast every morning, but porridge (clearly a dish she was not familiar with), accompanied by lukewarm ham and eggs swimming in olive oil and piles of toast and marmalade, is not the most suitable diet for a heatwave, especially when one is about to embark on a full-speed re-enactment of the Monaco Grand Prix in an aging Fiat with bald types. Those thousands of lire I spent on candles were clearly a very shrewd investment, as the only casualty during our entire visit was that stall selling watermelons on the way to the airport. I shall never forget that awful squishing sound — I was convinced it was the watermelon seller's head. I don't mean to sound ungrateful, but I'm glad we didn't get in touch before the second week of our holiday as I really don't think either my nerves or my digestion could have coped with a full fortnight of fried eggs and Fangio.

Yours sincerely,
Rowena Leadbetter

THE NINTH COMMANDMENT

THOU SHALT NOT PANIC AND GO OVER THE TOP

Gushing can have very unfortunate consequences; it may lead to accusations of sarcasm ('Anyone calling my collapsed soufflé and uncooked sprouts delicious must be taking the mickey') or, even worse, it can bring about an unwanted encore ('Thank God, I've finally discovered someone who finds my mother-in-law's company delightful').

THE TENTH COMMANDMENT

THOU SHALT PLAY SAFE

It is not a good idea to congratulate your hostess on her shepherd's pie when she has spent hours slaving over a hot moussaka, and disinheritance may well be the outcome of thanking Great Aunt Harriet for her 'very pretty indoor watering-can' when she has coughed up a Ming ewer. If in any doubt, seek refuge in generalities, bearing in mind, of course, that while a 'present' is always a 'present' (and *never* a 'gift'), a 'stew' is always a 'casserole'.

Never dine and whine.

Confucius, he say: man who dips pen in honey will find letter-writing a sticky business.

A bad bread-and-butter letter is like a bad bread-and-butter pudding: either dry and full of hot air or stodgy and indigestible.

The milk of human kindness is Milk of Amnesia.

Thanks are like boiled eggs: hard to swallow if overdone.

A thank-you letter is like cheap muesli: what it leaves out is much more interesting than what it contains.

Food

Food, most notably in the form of dinner parties, still
has the power to unleash a flood of thank-you letters.
Sometimes, of course, the grateful sentiments
expressed in these letters are entirely genuine, but just
occasionally there is more than a whiff of dishonesty in
the wind. . . In mitigation, however, it has to be said
that only the foolhardy, the terminally ill or those
about to emigrate should contemplate telling the
truth, the whole truth and nothing but the truth in the
aftermath of a true disaster. How, without reducing
your hostess to either blind fury or gibbering hysteria,
are you supposed to thank her for a party where the
quiche and the company were both equally half-
baked? There is no alternative but to lie back, think of
perfidious Albion and tell a series of whoppers.
Occasionally, however, if you're feeling particularly
hard done by, it is permissible to drop a few subtle
hints like 'the salad was delicious' (i.e. 'it was the only
edible thing') or 'Tim certainly has the most amazing
fund of stories' (i.e. 'your brother never drew breath
and bored us all rigid'). This technique is called
'writing between the lines' and is an invaluable device
for those whose delicate sensibilities will not allow
them to commit out-and-out perjury with a clear
conscience.

Dear Uncle Michael

Thank you very much for taking me out to lunch last Sunday and also for taking me to the museum. I enjoyed it very much. We played rugger at St Crispins yesterday and I scored a try. Next week we play against Cranbourne And I hope I shall be in the team. I hope you are well. Saunders who is in my dormitory has been sent to the San because he has mumps and he cant do his exams. Maton took my temperature today.

love from
william

Dear Uncle Michael,

I wanted to have a double hamburger and chips on Sunday and not go to a boring hotel and eat French things in slimy sauce. Uncle John has got a sports car and he takes me to McDonalds and then to the cinema and gives me lots of popcorn and coke which is super fun. He also gives me money. I dont like museums because they are boring and smelly. I kicked the head boy of St Crispins in the teeth and broke his plate because he called me a fat-face fool. Mr Whittle sent me off and said I cant play against Cranbourne, but I didnt want to anyway because they give us sardine sandwiches. Potts says that when his uncle got mumps his willy swelled up and Saunders is very worried.

Love from
William

Dear Mildred,

Thank you so much for the splendid Thanksgiving Day dinner I had at your house last week. I now understand why English people are always singing the praises of American hospitality. It was also great fun meeting all your family and I feel very honoured to have been included in the party. I hope you have a good holiday in Miami and I look forward to meeting you again soon. In the meantime, again many thanks for everything.

Yours,
Jonathan

Dear Mrs Gazornaplatt,

People in England warned me about the vast quantities of food consumed by Americans at Thanksgiving, but I never really believed them. Now I know they weren't exaggerating — never in the history of man's endeavour has so much been eaten by so few. I only wish I'd realized sooner that people in New Jersey don't seem to think it rude to leave food on their plates; after I'd waded through enough turkey to feed the poor of four parishes and your mother had overruled my feeble protests and presented me with a second food mountain (I do wish I'd known the Estonian for 'I hate sweet potatoes'), I seriously considered leaving the table and heading for the vomitorium. As it was, I had to make several comfort stops on the way back to New York to offload what my system will now always identify as 'stomach-pumpkin pie'. I didn't sleep a wink all night and could hardly drag myself into work the next day, but as I knew your husband would want to know why I wasn't in the office I've been spending 24 hours on the water biscuit and Alka-Seltzer diet (when he very kindly offered me a turkey sandwich I almost decorated my desk). I now feel like an overfilled wineskin (no wonder Americans are so keen on stretch trousers), but if you need a killer whale lookalike to scare the Florida sharks, I'm your man.

Yours,
Jonathan

Dear Julia,

Thank you very much for the splendid barbecue last Wednesday, which Louisa and I both enjoyed thoroughly. It was also great fun meeting all your new American friends; the next time you're over in England you must give us more warning so that we can arrange something. I hope you have a good journey back and do please keep in touch.

Yours,
Rodney

Dear Julia,

Bloody hell — a vegetarian barbecue and, even worse, not a sniff of booze. You might have had the decency to tell me you'd become a born-again Buddhist and then we could at least have stopped at a pub and had a few sandwiches. I've never seen so many nut cutlets and lentils in all my life. Louisa felt extremely unwell, but the only effect it had on me was to inflict such violent wind that I was forced to drive home with all the windows open and then made to move into the spare room. As if that weren't bad enough, it took me three times longer than normal to get into work this morning on the tube because I had to keep on getting out every second stop before people correctly identified the source of all those dreadful noises and their after-effects. My poor secretary only managed 3/4 hour before announcing that she had suddenly acquired a mysterious headache and could she please have the rest of the day off. Never again, I swear, will I eat another chick pea or soya bean, and never again will I waste three hours discussing the contemporary relevance of Taoism and the problems of the Nicaraguan peasant with a group of caftans and Clark's sandals. If that's what California does to people I'm quite happy to stick to Surrey.

Rodney

Dear Mary,
This is just a short note to say thank you very much from us both for the super buffet supper you gave last Wednesday, which we enjoyed enormously — you certainly did full justice to your new kitchen. I love the way you've redecorated the house — it looks wonderful. I just hope the place didn't look too much of a wreck after we'd all left! Again, many thanks for a most enjoyable evening.
Love,
Sally

Dear Mary,

Thank God I've got big writing as I really can't think of anything original to say about what was basically a pretty dire evening (I would've rung to say thank you, but I was warned that you're trying to organize a party for one of those dreadful charity balls in aid of incontinent gentlefolk). John and I both hate standing cheek by jowl with fifty other people trying to juggle quiche and salad like a poorly-trained troupe of circus plate-spinners, but at least the coleslaw was an exact match for your new flecked carpet. I only wish I could say the same of my dress. Incidentally, I recognized everything except the lettuce from my weekly visits to Marks & Sparks — why on earth did you bother spending a fortune on that new kitchen if you're not even going to use it? Beats me.

Love,
Sally

PS   I disclaim all responsibility for that brown stain on the carpet. It wasn't my fault: Paul stumbled over the dog, pushed Alice into Diana's cigarette and sent her screaming headlong into my wine-glass. I'm just sorry that the only way I could recover my balance was to grab hold of what without my contact lenses looked remarkably like part of the mantel-piece, but actually turned out to be a full bowl of meringues in chocolate sauce. Thank goodness most of it landed on Alice.

Dear Fatima,

Thank you so much for the super party that you gave last night. It was such a treat being taken out to a restaurant and having a change from the usual dinner party food. I've never tried Middle Eastern cooking before, but I can quite see now why Robert looks forward so much to his visits to the Gulf. It was also great fun meeting you and Ali after hearing so much about you, and I thought your parents were charming. We are off to the Dordogne soon, but we must try and get together again before you go back. Again many thanks for a truly memorable evening. Robert sends his regards and looks forward to seeing you in October.

Yours,
Patricia

Dear Fatima,

Please forgive my shaky handwriting, but I'm still suffering the after-effects of that extraordinary meal. Spicy food has never agreed with me, but there was something particularly virulent lurking in that rice dish which has made going to the loo both frequent and painful. I haven't been able to risk a visit to Sainsbury's for three days. How the Lebanese actually manage to eat that stuff seven days a week and still plant car bombs I shall never know; they must have stomachs of pure cast iron. No wonder Robert has become a kaolin and morphine addict. I only understood one word in four of what your father was saying as we have little experience of either falconry or camel racing in Haywards Heath, but your mother certainly knows her way around Bond Street and Knightsbridge. Robert had been banging on for weeks about me having to dress modestly, which is why I arrived in the restaurant looking like a nun on her way to inspect the convent beehives. I felt a complete twit. We're not in fact going to France for another fortnight, but I don't think my system could survive a second series of disturbed nights like the one I've just been through. We had the most flaming row on the way home, but I absolutely refuse to go through all that again, however desperate Robert is to get the contract for that new hospital.

Yours,
Patricia

Dear Vanessa,
Thank you so much for the picnic you gave on Gold Cup Day, which I enjoyed very much indeed. It was a pity that the weather wasn't on our side, but all that good food and drink more than compensated for it. I'm sorry we never managed to meet up again later, but I hope you had a successful day anyway. I actually left before the last race, a little poorer, but no wiser. Again many thanks for everything.

Yours,
  Hugo

Dear Vanessa,

Why do I have such a short memory? Your picnic this year was a perfect action replay of last year's wash-out, after which I had vowed 'Never again'. We stood in the same muddy grass like a clump of damp mushrooms, the women wearing the same silly hats and the men making the same ritual noises about the rain easing off. The heavens opened up right on cue and all the wet feathers promptly disappeared into the car like Mrs Noah's chickens, leaving me standing like Heathcliff clutching a plate of watery lettuce and soggy salmon. Have *you* ever tried carrying on a light-hearted conversation through a half-open window as rivulets of diluted mayonnaise course down your left leg? I don't recommend it. Thank God your chocolate mousse was still frozen solid. I spent the rest of the day hiding in a bar drinking brandy and trying to dry out. Never again! And this time I mean it.

Yours,
Hugo

Dear Camilla,
Thank you for the splendid dinner party on Monday; I'm just sorry that I arrived so late, but I got rather lost in Battersea. You really are a great cook; that soup was quite delicious, as was the main course. I enjoyed meeting your parents and also seeing Denise again after all these years and Tom, who I haven't seen since university. It was a most entertaining evening, for which again many thanks. I look forward to seeing you at Charlotte's on Thursday.

Yours,
Charles

Dear Camilla,

Why in God's name didn't you tell me your parents were going to be there? I was so pissed by the time I left Paddy's that finding my way to the bathroom, let alone to Battersea, posed major problems. As it was, I had God's own trouble trying to push all those bits of peanut down the bidet, but it did feel just like a loo in the dark. I shall never understand that extraordinary modern idea of having the light switch outside the door. I really don't remember much about the food at all, except for that revolting soup which looked like a stagnant pond: just what I didn't need when the room was starting to spin. I also had a good deal of trouble trying to follow your mother's ramblings about Rhodesia and the white man's burden; I just hope I didn't put my foot in it completely, but some of those African names, particularly ones like Sithole, are jolly hard to pronounce at the best of times. I always thought Tom was a complete cretin at Cambridge and he hasn't changed a bit: just because he and Denise went on safari in Kenya for their honeymoon doesn't mean that they're the world's authority on majority rule. I'm going to be on my best behaviour at Charlotte's and I shall take you out to dinner afterwards to make up for calling your sister and brother-in-law brainless Communists and for spewing up in your hedge on the way out.

Yours,
Charles

THE ELEVENTH COMMANDMENT

THOU SHALT NOT GO FOR THE JOCULAR

One man's wit is another man's poison and it is highly dangerous to assume that other people share your sense of humour. The prevailing tone of every thank-you letter should be one of polite gratitude, however restrained. In cases of extreme provocation, lock up your writing paper and kick the cat.

THE TWELFTH COMMANDMENT

THOU SHALT SOUND CONVINCING

If the recipient of a thank-you letter should happen to smell a rat, then the writer of that letter is in serious trouble. It is therefore best to avoid unnecessary superlatives and palpable lies. Beware of underestimating your reader's intelligence: it is an unfortunate fact of life that colour-blind misers and uncouth peasants are not necessarily stupid. They may of course be illiterate, but that's not a gamble worth taking.

'On the Thirteenth Day of Christmas
my parents gave to me...
a pen and said
"Have you written your
thank-you letters yet?"

The present

For children, thank-you letters form an integral part of the Christmas ritual: like cold turkey and reheated mince pies, they are the sting in the tail of the festive season. By early January, postboxes all over the country are filled with envelopes covered in spidery writing containing laboriously-crafted expressions of thanks for presents that have frequently been either broken or surreptitiously consigned to the darkest recesses of the toy cupboard, only to reemerge in time for the next jumble sale. These childhood bread-and-butter letters (an expression that itself reveals the degree of relish with which they are undertaken) set the tone for all future thank-you letters: they are written out of a sense of duty and, more often than not, they tread a very fine line between politeness and appalling insincerity. They are an early introduction to that necessary social evil, the white lie, and children who for eleven months of the year have had their ears boxed for not telling the truth suddenly find themselves being forced by their parents to go into ersatz raptures over presents that very often leave them completely cold. It does, however, provide excellent practice for later life, when the same technique used to thank for some boring book on wild flowers (when all you wanted was a pet monkey) can be applied to thanking great aunt Maud for the floral-pattern wastepaper basket (the eleventh one received so far) she has so kindly sent for your wedding.

'It is an art to have so much judgement as to apparel a lie well, to give it a good dressing'.

BEN JOHNSON, *Explorata: Mali Choragi Fuere*

79

Dear Uncle George,

Thank you very much for the wedding present that you gave me and Susan. It was much appreciated by us both, particularly as Susan is a Cordon Bleu cook. I am so glad you were able to come to the reception; I'm just sorry I didn't get more time to speak to you, but you know how it is at weddings! We really must try and keep in touch. Susan and I have just returned from two weeks in the Maldives, where we had a wonderful time snorkelling and just lazing about. Susan is absolutely black! Again many thanks for your present and I look forward to seeing you again soon.

Yours,
Ian.

Dear Uncle George,

You're my only godparent still alive and you're also stinking rich, so when you asked me whether we'd like a food mixer as a wedding present I didn't expect one of those bloody manual jobs. I suggested to Susan that she take a Cordon Bleu course, with the idea of sending her out to do director's lunches — she, poor soul, thought it was just so that she could give endless dinner parties! Anyway, a fat lot of help that flaming present of yours is going to be in paying off the mortgage. My mother says you're eccentric, but I say you're just bloody mean. We had a fortnight of hell in the Maldives — the only place I was safe from the flies was under the water and Susan got so badly burnt that she had to spend the last week in bed shedding three layers of skin and stinking of Calomine. What was even worse was that she'd been sunbathing topless and got so sore that I couldn't lay a finger on her. Some bloody honeymoon that was. Thanks for nothing.

Ian

Dear uncle Gerald,

Thank you very much for the book token which you gave me for chrismas. I had a grate chrismas and got lots of presents. I am going to by a book about moddeling. I hope you had a good chrismas. I am going to Arabella's party on wensday

Love from Ronald.

Dear Uncle Gerald,
You are a boring old fart. I hate books and the sisstant in Smiths would not let me by tapes. Anyway, how many tapes can you by for five pounds you old skintflint so I bort the Playboy annual. I bet you thort I was going to make stupid old plastic models of Concorde. I took the Playboy book to Arabella's party and her farther confisskatered it. He was jellus because Arabella's mother has got small buzums. I have arsked Mum to get you to by record tokens next time.

Ronald

Dear Aunt Susan,

   Thank you very much for the dolly you gave me for Christmas. It is super and I play with it a lot. Charles and I are going to the Pantymime on Saterday. We had a lovely Christmas and I got a lot of Presents. Baby Charles had second helpings of christmas pudding and was sick

   Love from Sophie

Dear Aunt Susan,

I didnt want to rite you a letter, but Mummy made me. You are a complete wolly. I am six years old and I hate stupid dolls. My best frend Sarah told me about a super video she had seen with her brother called Multipel Massaccre and so we shaved its head with Daddy's lectric razer and then stuck it in Mummy's Magimix with a tube of rasberry topping but we broke the razer and the Magimix. Then baby Charles chued off one of its legs and was sick and now Daddy has stopped my poket money. It's all your stupid fault and I hate you.

Sophie

To Her Most Serene Highness
the Sultana of Rumgoolie

Her Majesty
graciously acknowledges receipt
of the present
sent by Your Most Serene Highness
to mark the occasion of
her fifty-ninth birthday
and bids me express
her grateful thanks.
    Your obedient servant,

Ronald Firkington-Twytte KBE
(Chief Keeper of the Cellars)

Dear Raisin-Face,

We have not the faintest idea who you are, but we think your present smells. We have no use in our palace for a cruet-stand made of inlaid brass and antelope's legs and we have therefore filed it under U.G. (Unbelievably Ghastly) and consigned it to our basement. It now rests between the Union Jack leg warmers, hand-crocheted by Mrs Ada Thatcher of 4, Tebbitt's Bottom, Batley, and sent to our mother on the occasion of her eightieth birthday, and the pickled giraffe's penis, narrowly rescued from our corgis, presented to us by the Chief Bong of Bogi to mark our younger son's attainment of manhood. We are rapidly running out of space in our basement and may shortly be obliged to make an anonymous donation to our local Oxfam Shop.

Dear Aunt Sophie,

You have probably heard that my engagement to Roger has been called off and so I'm afraid that I have to return your wedding present. It is, however, an extremely pretty cachepot and I should like to thank you very much for having sent it — it was a very kind thought. As you can imagine, this is rather a difficult time for the family but I'm sure it's all for the best in the long run. Again, many thanks and we must meet for lunch soon.

Much love,
Venetia

Dear Aunt Sophie,

Daddy always said I was a lousy judge of character and he's absolutely delighted the whole thing's off. He says he's going to take Mummy on a decent holiday with all the money he's saved, but he refuses point-blank to send the champagne back and spends most of the day completely sozzled, thanking God for a narrow escape. I must say one of the consolations of a broken engagement is being able to send back all those ghastly presents that were quite obviously either recycled or bought half-price in the spring sales. After having some people tell me to keep theirs I've now learned my lesson and started returning the worst ones (pink and mauve cachepots included) before I get landed with them for ever. See you soon,

Much love,
Venetia

PS I hope you've managed to offload that dreadful thing before I make my next stab at matrimony.

When writing a thank-you letter, NEVER use any words beginning with *re* (as in -pulsive, -volting, -luctant or, even worse, -gurgitate, -ptilian and -tch) or *di* (as in -gestion, -arrhoea, -sgusting, -sappointing and -seased).

Lying low

(there *is* an alternative)

ıg = a, restful ('a wonderfully restful weekend'
= 'we were reduced to rereading back
numbers of *Country Life* at least twice')
b, fascinating ('your uncle is a fascinating
person' = 'he bores for Europe')

eakable = a, pleasant ('nettle tea certainly makes a
pleasant change from coffee' = 'I'm
responsible for the sudden death of all your
African violets')

b, original ('what an original idea to cook Indonesian food' = 'and you know what you can do with your wok...')

useless = a, useful ('your ice mould is going to be so useful' = 'Who is going to be stupid enough to buy *this* at the church fête?')

b, helpful ('Daniel is extremely helpful in the kitchen' = 'your son breaks everything he touches')

ugly = a, beautiful ('the beautiful green and mauve bathmat you gave us' = 'there goes another contribution to the White Elephant stall')

b, wonderful ('that wonderful flock wall-paper' = 'Very Sandersons, very Tandoori')

idiotic = a, clever ('you have been so clever with the new dining room' = 'where do you get your taste from? Your feet?')

b, splendid ('your aunt really is a splendid character' = 'she should be locked up immediately')

uncomfortable = a, welcome ('you and your husband made us feel so welcome' = 'even the Borgias offered their guests something to drink')

b, comfortable ('the spare room was so comfortable' = 'there were even more lumps in the bed than in the porridge')

indescribable = a, delicious ('that delicious casserole we had' = 'the last time I saw pieces of meat like that was in a biology practical')

b, ingenious ('that ingenious gadget you gave us for the kitchen' = 'I am unable to repeat any of the suggestions as to what that extraordinary implement could be used for')

disastrous = a, memorable ('a truly memorable dinner party' = 'the memory, like the heartburn, lingers on')

b, unforgettable ('an unforgettable weekend down in Dorset' = 'my idea of Hell is three rainy days trapped in a suburb of Bognor')

inedible = a, wonderful ('those wonderful brains in aspic' = 'does *cuisine minceur* mean throwing up to keep thin?')

b, fascinating ('that fascinating pudding' = 'it looked just like something you'd punish the dog for')

frightful = a, super ('the super ornament' = 'a ceramic tit perched on a sprig of pink apple blossom')

b, marvellous ('a marvellous fireworks party' = 'four rockets, two burnt sausages and hypothermia')

93

Headline books are available at your bookshop or newsagent, or can be ordered from the following address:

Headline Book Publishing PLC
Cash Sales Department
PO Box 11
Falmouth
Cornwall
TR10 9EN
England

UK customers please send cheque or postal order (no currency), allowing 60p for postage and packing for the first book, plus 25p for the second book and 15p for each additional book ordered up to a maximum charge of £1.90 in UK.

BFPO customers please allow 60p for postage and packing for the first book, plus 25p for the second book and 15p per copy for the next seven books, thereafter 9p per book.

Overseas and Eire customers please allow £1.25 for postage and packing for the first book, plus 75p for the second book and 28p for each subsequent book.